Tomáš Míček
Elisabeth Kellner

LIPIZZANER HORSES

Text by
Dr. Hans-Jörg Schrenk

SUNBURST BOOKS

Maestoso Bonavajo-45, a stallion from the Lipica Stud, observes the photographer in the calm, placid way that is typical of his breed.

*These mares are in a hurry to get to the paddock, eagerly anticipating
the freedom of the meadow.*

A herd of mares on the Dakovo Stud.

The mares and foals spend all day out in the meadows, and are only brought back to the stables when the weather is very hot.

Every horse-lover who has seen them is captivated by the grey stallions of the Spanish Riding School in Vienna. A gala performance at the Hofburg is an unforgettable experience for any admirer of dressage and beautiful horses. Watching the Lipizzaner stallions performing haute école figures such as the *quadrille* or the *pas de deux* of two stallions, with their riders dressed in brown tails, is evocative of the Baroque era.

The Lipizzaners are probably one of the oldest breeds of horse in the world. They have been bred specifically for the Spanish Riding School for over 400 years. The Viennese stallions are bred at the Austrian national stud of Piber in Styria. Following a successful career at the Spanish Riding School, the stallions return to Piber to be used for breeding.

The stallion Favory Gaetana, born in 1975, enjoys a race around the paddock at the Dakovo Stud.

Tulipan Zenta from the Tulipan line of horses releases all his pent-up energy in a series of wild leaps and gallops after standing in his stall for a long time.

The Spanish Riding School stallions are all bred at the Piber Stud. But there are also Lipizzaner studs in many of the countries which used to be part of the former Austro-Hungarian Empire. Lipica (also known as Lipizza), the birth place of the Lipizzaner breed, became the Yugoslavian national stud. The Lipizzaner stud of Dakovo is also in Yugoslavia. Elsewhere in the region there is the Hungarian Lipizzaner stud at Szilvasvarad, the Fagaras Stud in Romania and an Italian stud at Monterodondo near Rome. Lipizzaners are also bred in Czechoslovakia, where the main stud is called Topolcianky.

Tomáš Míček and Elisabeth Kellner have visited most of these studs to photograph the Lipizzaners for this book.

This foal is just a few days old and still has its greyish-brown foal's coat. The final colour of the Lipizzaner's coat can only be determined when the horse is fully mature, at the age of 5-7.

A mare and her foal in the pastures of Lipica. The first white hairs have appeared at the side of the foal's nostrils.

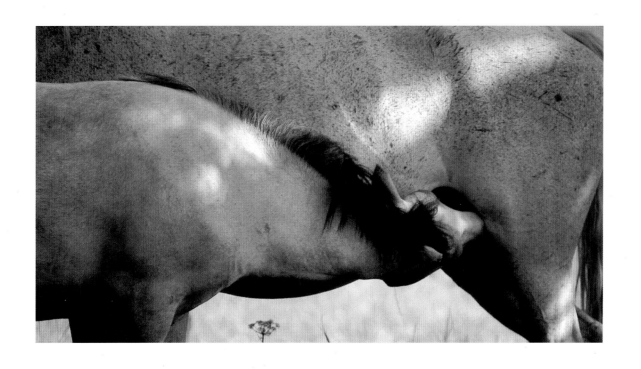

The foal always comes back to its mother to drink, no matter how rich the pasture is.

In the Baroque age the Spanish horses were considered to be the best thoroughbred riding and carriage horses, and ownership of these horses was a status symbol in all the royal courts of Europe. The Spanish horses, also known as Andalusians, were a cross between the heavy, native Spanish horses and the horses of the Berbers of Arabia, who came to Spain in the 8th century, when Spain was conquered by the Moors. One feature which the Lipizzaners inherited from the Arab horses was the roman nose, which was a distinctive characteristic of the Lipizzaners until the turn of the century. When it eventually became too expensive and dangerous to import horses for the royal stables directly from Spain, many courts began to establish their own studs, such as that at Frederiksborg in Denmark, or the royal Austrian stud of Kladrub in Bohemia. In 1580 Archbishop Karl II, the ruler of what was at that time still an Austrian province on the Adriatic Sea, founded a stud in the small village of Lipica, about 25 kilometres from the coast. In the same year 9 stallions and 24 mares were imported from Spain as the initial stock for breeding parade-horses for the imperial court in Vienna. These Andalusians were crossed with the strong, stocky, native horses, whose endurance and strength had been praised since Roman times. Another ancestor of the Lipizzaner was the Neapolitan, a cross between Andalusian and Arab, which was popular during the Baroque era because of its slow, high-stepping gait - the so-called Spanish gait. At first the stud of Lipica bred mainly the multi-coloured horses that were popular at the time, such as piebalds, skewbalds and dapples. It was only in the early 19th century, when, for a while, an increased number of thoroughbred Arabs were used for breeding Lipizzaners, that the grey colour became the hallmark of the Lipizzaner. Nowadays, as well as the greys, one also occasionally sees bay Lipizzaners.

The mares from the Monterotondo Stud in Italy. These mares spend all year out at grass, and are not used for riding or driving.

*At full gallop in
the paddock*

Since the 18th century the Lipizzaner has been bred from six classic lines, which can be traced back to the following stallions: the grey stallion Pluto, born in 1765, from the stud of Frederiksborg in Denmark, which breeds magnificent horses from Spanish and Neapolitan stallions. The two stallions Conversano, born in 1767, and Neapolitano, born in 1790, are Neapolitans who were imported from Italy. The stallions Maestoso, a grey who was born in 1773, and Favory, a dun born in 1779, from the royal stud of Kladrub, which also used Spanish horses for breeding. The Arab stallion, Siglavy, was the founder of a line of lighter, more finely built Lipizzaners. Siglavy was born in 1810 and imported to Lipica in 1816. Two other significant lines, although they are not included in the classic lineage, are those of Tulipan and Incitato, which stem from Croatia and Siebenbürgen.

The young stallion Maestoso Gaetana XIV, born in 1986.

The stud of Lipica has a colourful history. The horses at Lipica often had to be evacuated to protect them from attack during wartime. In 1797 the herd was rescued from the approaching French army and set out on a forty day march to Hungary. After six months the horses returned to Lipica. But in 1805 they had to leave their home once again. Through ice and snow the horses were moved to Dakovo in Slovenia, where they stayed for two years before their return in 1807. In 1809 they were evacuated again, this time to Mezöhegyes in Hungary, where they remained until 1815. The Second World War just about put an end to the breeding of Lipizzaners. The horses from the studs of Lipica, Piber and Demir Kapija were rounded up and held by the German army in Hostau in Bohemia, and it was only thanks to the combined efforts of the director of the Spanish riding school in Vienna, the manager of the stud of Hostau and the American General, George Patton, that the herd of around 300 survived the threat of the approaching Russian front.

Another view of the imposing head of the stallion Maestoso Bonavoja-45. He was born in Lipica in 1967.

Apart from the original stud of Lipica, which was founded in 1580, a number of other studs have been established over the last 200 years to continue the heritage of the Lipizzaner. Some of the horses evacuated from Lipica in 1809 remained in Mezöhegyes and were subsequently used for breeding there. But because the Lipizzaners did not thrive as well on the lowlands of Hungary as they did on the high plateau of Lipica, the Hungarian national stud of Fagaras was established in 1874, and the Lipizzaners from Mezöhegyes were transferred there. In 1912 the stud was moved to Babolna, and then again to its present location in Szilvasvarad. Nowadays the Szilvasvarad Stud breeds Lipizzaners as resilient, high-performance carriage and draught horses for agricultural use. In international trotting competitions the Lipizzaners from Szilvasvarad have already won many prizes. During the First World War the stud of Lipica was moved to Laxenburg near Vienna, and some of the animals were moved to the stud of Kladrub in Bohemia. With these horses, who were in Czechoslovakia in 1918, the Czech Lipizzaner stud of Topolcianky was founded in 1921.

Siglavy Bonadea XIII, born 1984 in Dakovo.

In 1918, after the First World War, the region where the stud of Lipica was located became a part of Italy. The Lipizzaners that had been kept temporarily at Laxenburg near Vienna were divided up between Italy and Austria. The Italian horses were returned to Lipica, and, in 1920, the Austrian government opened a stud in Piber, Styria, which supplies Lipizzaners to the Spanish Riding School in Vienna to this day. In 1942 the stocks from both Piber and Lipica were confiscated by the German army and moved to the stud of Hostau in Bohemia. After the Second World War these horses were divided up between Italy, Yugoslavia and Austria. Yugoslavia then inherited the Lipica Stud and continued to breed Lipizzaners there. Italy established its own Lipizzaner stud in Monterotondo near Rome, and the Austrian Lipizzaners were returned to Piber. The stud in Lipica has, in the meantime, become a popular tourist attraction, and riding and carriage driving courses are held there. The school stallions are still trained in the figures of the haute école and perform their skills in dressage events.

The mare, Aurica-27, looks suspiciously at the photographer.

These mares, Aurica-27 and Madera-69, both from Piber, are now kept at a private stud in Going, Austria.

Initially, the Italian stud of Monterotondo was run by the ministry of defence, before being handed over to the ministry of agriculture. Today this Lipizzaner stud is being run as a "wild" stud: the mares are kept in groups out in the pastures; every spring, at the start of the breeding season, a stallion is allocated to each of these small herds to cover the mares. The mares are not broken for riding or driving. The only human contact with them is when they are fed - their natural diet is supplemented by high-energy fodder - and when they are treated by the vet.

There is another stud in Yugoslavia in addition to Lipica - the stud of Dakovo in Croatia - which breeds Lipizzaners mainly as work horses. These horses are ideally suited to agricultural work, as they are heavier and smaller than the school horses from Lipica and Piber. The Dakovo stock originates mainly from the former Yugoslav state-owned stud of Stanic, and comprises about 40 brood mares and 60 stallions.

Romania also has a stud, which was established in 1920 on the former Hungarian stud of Fagaras. There are about 120 mares there. At this stud the Lipizzaners are bred primarily as work horses, many of which are used for cross-breeding in Romania.

Great things are expected of Siglavy Vera XI, one of the young stallions born in 1986 at Lipica.

Pluto Verona-16 from Piber, now privately owned by the Stangl-Wirts from Going in the Tyrol.

Right: A portrait of Pluto Verona-16, who was born in 1973 and has proved to be an extremely successful stud stallion.

The days of the Lipizzaner as the parade horse of the royal courts were over long ago. With its powerful neck and massive build it is ideally suited to the figures of the haute école, but not really to dressage. The Lipizzaner rarely competes at dressage events, for it has a different gait to that of the thoroughbreds, which makes it difficult for the judges to compare performances. However, it is an ideal horse for leisure riders, especially those with dressage ambitions. Good-natured and intelligent, it is a versatile all-round horse. It is particularly successful in driving competitions, as demonstrated by the Hungarian carriage-and-four champion, György Bardos, and his Lipizzaner team on several occasions. In Hungary the Lipizzaner is crossed with trotters to improve its chances in international races.

Pluto Batosta, born in 1984 in Dakova, at full gallop in the paddock.

Two young stallions from the herd at Dakova stare curiously at the photographer.

*Favory Zenta, born in 1983 in Dakova, demonstrates the
powerful elegance of this ancient breed.*

The mares of Monterotondo move slowly across the wide expanses of pasture at Emilia Romagna in the evening sun.

Krabbe, a flea-bitten grey mare at the Dakova Stud.

A herd of mares at the Lipica Stud.

Pluto Verona-16 again. This old stallion from Piber has already earned a reputation at the Spanish Riding School.

Maestoso Caprice-50, who was born in 1977, also comes from Piber stock.
He, too, has demonstrated his abilities at the Spanish Riding School in
Vienna. In contrast, out in the open, he enjoys rolling in the snow.

Pluto Verona-16